LETHAL TRANSACTIONS

RAVITEJA MUREBOINA

CONTENTS

1.ENTREPRENEURIAL JOURNEY

Venkatesh is a hardworking individual who has a strong work ethic and is willing to put in the necessary effort to achieve his goals. He is driven and persistent, which has helped him to succeed in business despite facing many hardships along the way. Despite the setbacks and failures, he has encountered in his entrepreneurial journey, Venkatesh has a never-give-up attitude and continues to persevere until he achieves success.

In addition to his strong work ethic and perseverance, Venkatesh also has a helping nature. He is always willing to lend a helping hand to those in need, whether it be his employees, friends, or family members. He believes in the importance of giving back to society and making a positive impact in the world.

Venkatesh is also known for being a serial entrepreneur, having started multiple businesses throughout his career. Although some of these ventures may have failed, he never gave up and continued to learn from his mistakes, which ultimately led to the success of his company. His ability to adapt and learn from his failures has been a key factor in his success.

Overall, Venkatesh is a determined, hardworking, and compassionate individual who has achieved success through his perseverance, willingness to help others, and never-give-up attitude.

During his journey as an entrepreneur, Venkatesh met Kajal, a friendly, hardworking, and outgoing person. It was during one of his business trips that Venkatesh met Kajal, and the two quickly became good friends. As they spent more time together, they discovered that they had much in common and started to develop feelings for each other.

After some time, Venkatesh and Kajal decided to get married in 2001. The wedding was a grand affair, with all the family members and friends gathering to celebrate the union of this beautiful couple. The wedding was well organized, with everything from the decorations to the food being planned and executed to perfection.

For Venkatesh and Kajal, their marriage was a partnership built on mutual respect, love, and hard work. They supported each other through all the ups and downs of life, and they worked tirelessly to build a life together. Kajal's outgoing and friendly nature helped Venkatesh to expand his business network and make new connections in the industry.

As they settled into married life, Venkatesh and Kajal's bond only grew stronger. They faced many challenges, but with each obstacle, they emerged stronger and more committed to each other. Together, they built a beautiful family and a successful business. Venkatesh's journey may have been a difficult one, but with Kajal by his side, he knew he could conquer anything.

The expansion was not easy for Venkatesh, as he faced several challenges along the way. There were financial constraints, regulatory hurdles, and intense competition in his industry. However, Venkatesh remained determined and focused on his goals, and he was able to overcome these challenges.

One of the reasons for Venkatesh's success was his ability to establish a good network in his business. He knew that he could not do everything alone, and he needed to work with others to achieve his goals. Therefore, he built strong relationships with his clients, suppliers, and employees.

Venkatesh's network was not limited to just his business contacts. He also established connections with other entrepreneurs, industry experts, and mentors. These relationships provided him with valuable insights, advice, and support, which helped him make informed decisions and navigate the challenges of running a business.

Venkatesh's success also came from his willingness to learn and adapt. He was always looking for ways to improve his business and stay ahead of the competition. He invested in new technology, expanded his services, and diversified his client base. These strategies helped him grow his business and establish a strong presence in the market.

2. THE ARRIVAL OF A NEWLY BORN

The birth of a child is one of the most beautiful and precious moments in a person's life, and for Venkatesh, the arrival of his son Raj in January 2005 was a moment he would never forget. Venkatesh had always been a hardworking and dedicated individual, but the birth of his son gave him a new sense of purpose and meaning. When he first laid eyes on his newborn son, Venkatesh was overcome with emotion and cried tears of joy. For him, seeing his child for the first time was a moment of pure happiness and fulfillment.

As the news of the birth of Raj spread throughout the family, there was a great sense of excitement and joy. When the family members finally got to meet the new addition to the family, they were immediately struck by his beauty and innocence. They knew that this child was special and would bring good luck to their family.

Venkatesh and Kajal were proud parents and wanted to choose a name that reflected their hopes and dreams for their son. They chose the name Raj, which means king, reflecting their belief that their son would one day rule his own business empire. From the moment of his birth, Raj was surrounded by the love and support of his family, and he grew up in a household filled with warmth and positivity.

As Raj grew up, he showed a natural talent for business, just like his father. He was a smart and ambitious young man, and he was always eager to learn more about the world of entrepreneurship. Venkatesh and Kajal were proud of their son and were thrilled to see him follow in his father's footsteps. They knew that with his talent and dedication, Raj was destined for great things.

As Raj turned one year old, he was already showing signs of being a happy and active child. He loved to explore the world around him and was always eager to learn new things.

Meanwhile, Venkatesh and his wife Kajal were working hard to expand their business. Despite the challenges they faced along the way, Venkatesh and Kajal remained determined and focused. They worked long hours, attended networking events, and constantly sought out new opportunities to grow their business.

One day, Venkatesh came home to find his wife playing with their son Raj. As he watched them, he realized that his family was what motivated him to work hard every day. He wanted to create a better future for his son and provide for his family.

With this newfound motivation, Venkatesh and Kajal redoubled their efforts to expand their business. They invested in new equipment, hired more staff, and expanded their services to meet the needs of their growing customer base.

As their business continued to thrive, Venkatesh and Kajal made sure to prioritize their family time. They took Raj on trips and spent weekends together as a family. They knew that their success in business was only meaningful if it allowed them to enjoy their lives to the fullest.

Years passed, and Raj grew into a bright and curious child. Venkatesh and Kajal's businesses continued to thrive, and they were able to provide a comfortable life for their family. As they looked back on their journey, they realized that the key to their success was their unwavering determination, hard work, and love for their family.

Venkatesh had built a successful business, but like many other businesses, he was hit by an economic crisis that threatened to bring it all down. Venkatesh was in a state of stress, unsure of what to do next. His wife, Kajal, tried to calm him down and reassure him that they would find a way to make it through this tough time. They both knew that it wouldn't be easy, but they were willing to do whatever it took to keep their business afloat.

As days passed, they received some good news. They had landed a deal with a company in the UK, which could potentially turn their business around. It was a big opportunity, but it came with its own set of challenges. Venkatesh and Kajal had to leave for the UK the next day to make the deal successful. They had just seven days to complete the meeting and seal the deal.

Despite the stress and uncertainty of the situation, Venkatesh and Kajal were determined to make the most of the opportunity. They prepared meticulously, studying the UK market and the company they were going to meet. They worked out a plan of action and set off to the UK with hope in their hearts.

The seven days in the UK were intense. Venkatesh and Kajal worked long hours, putting their best foot forward in every meeting. They made sure to build strong relationships with the company's representatives, understanding their needs and offering solutions that could benefit both parties.

It wasn't easy, but Venkatesh and Kajal persevered. They put all their effort into making the deal successful, and in the end, it paid off. The UK company was impressed with their professionalism and dedication, and they agreed to sign the deal.

With the deal done, Venkatesh and Kajal returned home, feeling a sense of relief and accomplishment. The business was back on track, and they had overcome the economic crisis that had threatened to bring them down. It wasn't just about the success of the deal; it was also about the perseverance and resilience they had shown in the face of adversity.

Raj had always been an observant child. Growing up, he watched his father work tirelessly to establish and grow his business. He saw the long hours, the stress, and the struggles his father faced every day. But he also saw the pride and satisfaction that came with owning and running a successful business.

As Raj grew older, he began to realize that he wanted to be a part of that world. He wanted to support his father's business and help it grow even further. So, he started researching and learning everything he could about the industry and the business.

He spent countless hours poring over books, attending seminars, and talking to experts in the field. He even worked part-time at his father's business, learning the ins and outs of the operation and gaining valuable experience.

As he gained more knowledge and expertise, Raj became more confident in his abilities. He knew that he had what it took to take his father's business to the next level.

At 19 years old, Raj was appointed as the CEO by his father. This was no small feat, as the company was already successful and had been around for several years. Raj was now responsible for leading and expanding the business, and he took the responsibility very seriously. He knew that he had big shoes to fill, but he was ready for the challenge.

Raj threw himself into his work, spending countless hours learning about the industry and coming up with innovative ideas to take the company to the next level. He was determined to make a name for himself and to ensure that the family business continued to thrive for generations to come.

One of the first things that Raj did was to streamline the company's operations. He identified areas where the business was wasting time and money and made changes to increase efficiency. This allowed the company to produce more products at a lower cost, which helped to increase profits.

Raj also focused on expanding the company's reach by exploring new markets and developing new products. He was always on the lookout for new opportunities and was not afraid to take risks. This led to the company's rapid growth, with new branches opening in different parts of the country.

Despite his young age, Raj was respected by his colleagues and employees alike. He had a clear vision for the company and was able to inspire others to work towards that vision. He was also approachable and always willing to listen to feedback and ideas from others.

Raj's hard work and dedication paid off, and the company continued to grow and thrive under his leadership. By the time he was in his mid-20s, the company had become a major player in the industry and had expanded globally.

Looking back on his journey, Raj credits his success to his willingness to learn and his determination to succeed. He knew that being named CEO at such a young age was a huge responsibility, but he also saw it as an opportunity to make a difference and leave a lasting legacy.

3.A SUDDEN TURN OF EVENTS

On 20th January 2010, the leak of sensitive information internally had a significant impact on the company, resulting in financial losses and a gradual decrease in stock prices. The situation was particularly challenging for the company's CEO, who was responsible for leading the organization through this difficult time. He had to navigate the fallout of the leak while trying to stabilize the company's finances and restore trust with its customers and investors. It was a hard time for everyone involved, and it required strong leadership and decisive action to overcome the crisis and set the company back on a path to success.

Raj had been working tirelessly to revive the fortunes of his family's company, but when he returned home, he was greeted with devastating news. He discovered that his father had passed away and found a note left behind that mentioned his father's concern over the company's future. The note mentioned how he couldn't bear the thought of witnessing the downfall of the company, and this made the situation even more difficult for Raj. It was a heartbreaking moment for Raj, and he was left feeling lost and alone without his father's guidance. However, he knew that he had to stay strong and continue to work hard to keep the company afloat.

The funeral activities had started, and people from all walks of life had come to pay their respects to Raj's father. Amongst them was Charan, one of the biggest enemies of the company, who had come with his wife, Deepika, and daughter, Anu, to offer their condolences. Raj observed a cunning smile on Charan's face as if he was feeling that there was no competitor for him now that Raj's father was no longer there to lead the company. Raj felt a surge of anger and resentment towards Charan, but he knew that this was not the time or the place to confront him. Instead, he made a mental note to keep a watchful eye on Charan's actions and intentions towards the company in the future. Despite the challenging circumstances, Raj remained focused on his father's funeral and ensuring that it was a dignified farewell to a great man who had left an indelible mark on the company and the community.

Despite their different roles in the company, Varun, Mahesh, Karthik, and Ajay were all taking on the responsibility of funeral activities for Raj's father. Varun, the driver, was helping to organize transportation for guests, while Mahesh, the gardener, was helping to set up the funeral venue. Karthik, who had been Raj's father's personal assistant, was helping to coordinate with vendors and guests, while Ajay, the vice president of the company, was ensuring that everything ran smoothly. It was heartening to see these individuals come together to support Raj during this difficult time, putting aside their differences and working towards a common goal. As they worked tirelessly to ensure that the funeral arrangements were perfect, Raj felt grateful for their dedication and support, and he knew that his father would be proud of the team that he had assembled.

4.THE FACT OF DEATH

Raj was convinced that his father's death was not a suicide, and he decided to take action by filing a complaint with the police. The police began their investigation, and as they delved deeper into the case, they discovered that the note left behind by Raj's father was not written by him, according to expert analysis. This discovery further fueled Raj's suspicion that his father's death was not a suicide but rather a premeditated act by someone else. As the investigation continued, Raj was hopeful that the truth would be uncovered and justice would be served for his father, who had dedicated his life to building the company and supporting his family.

During the investigation into his father's death, the police asked Raj if he had any doubts about anyone who could have been involved. Raj immediately mentioned Charan, who was a major competitor in their business. Raj suspected that Charan might have benefited from his father's death, as Charan's company profits had increased significantly since then. Raj believed that Charan might have been involved in his father's death as a way to eliminate competition and gain an advantage in the industry.

When the police questioned Raj about other people who might have been involved in his father's death, he stated that he had no doubts about anyone else. He vouched for Nithin, who was a dedicated and hardworking employee who always completed his projects on time. Although Nithin was financially struggling, Raj did not suspect him of any wrongdoing. Raj also praised Ajay, the vice president of the company, for making many good decisions that had contributed to the company's success. Similarly, Karthik, who was his father's personal assistant and close confidant, had no reason to harm his father. However, Raj was uncertain about Varun and Mahesh, who were new employees and did not have a long history with the company or his father. The police took note of Raj's comments and continued to investigate all potential leads in the case and look for any evidence that might link Charan to the crime.

Upon inquiry, it was discovered that Mahesh was on leave on the day Venkatesh passed away as he was attending his daughter's wedding. As for Varun, everyone who was questioned spoke highly of him. However, when the police dug deeper and examined his bank records, they discovered a sudden credit of 2 lakhs, which raised suspicions. Thus, Varun became the next person of interest in the investigation following Charan.

The following day, the investigation team initiated their inquiry by questioning Charan, who was a prominent business rival of Venkatesh. Raj, Venkatesh's son, had already expressed his doubts regarding Charan to Kumar, the senior investigating officer. Upon hearing this, Kumar confronted Charan with fervor and demanded to know the truth behind Venkatesh's demise. Charan denied any involvement in the murder and revealed that he had made several attempts to hinder Venkatesh's business ventures in the past. He also questioned why he would commit such a heinous crime, knowing that it would only harm his own company's reputation.

Through his sources, Kumar discovered that Charan had a previous engagement with Venkatesh's wife, Kajal, which was called off when they found out that Charan was only interested in the marriage for Kajal's business connections. Moreover, Charan was known to have employed underhanded tactics in the business arena, such as shutting down small businesses that posed a threat to his company. He also had informants in rival companies who would provide him with confidential information. This led Kumar to view Charan as a more likely suspect in Venkatesh's murder, given his history of deceit and ruthless tactics in the business world.

Further investigation by Kumar revealed that Charan had harbored resentment towards Venkatesh in the past. When Venkatesh had secured a deal with a company from the UK, Charan was reportedly furious as he was a competitor for the same deal and lost out to Venkatesh. This fueled Charan's animosity towards Venkatesh, which could have been a motive for him to commit the murder. With this new piece of information, Kumar was able to build a stronger case against Charan, and he made it his top priority to uncover any evidence that would link Charan to Venkatesh's death.

After questioning Charan, Kumar moved on to investigate other potential suspects, namely Nithin, Karthik, and Ajay. Upon looking into Ajay's background, Kumar found that he had a stellar track record within the company. Under his leadership, the company's stock prices had risen by an impressive 40%, indicating his ability to make sound business decisions. Ajay had started as a regular employee and had worked his way up to become a Vice President, displaying an admirable level of determination and dedication.

Karthik, on the other hand, had worked as Venkatesh's personal assistant for over 15 years and was known for his unwavering loyalty towards him. Kumar recognized that Karthik had a unique insight into Venkatesh's professional and personal life, making him a valuable source of information for the investigation. However, his unwavering loyalty to Venkatesh made him an unlikely suspect in the case.

Nithin was another potential suspect, and Kumar discovered that he had come from humble beginnings and was financially underprivileged. Despite this, Nithin's strong work ethic and exceptional knowledge had earned him a good position within the company. Kumar recognized Nithin's potential motive for committing the crime, as the financial gain from Venkatesh's position could have been a significant incentive. With this in mind, Kumar made it his mission to thoroughly investigate each of these individuals to uncover any evidence that could lead to Venkatesh's killer. Knowing all this information Kumar didn't suspect the murder.

After investigating Ajay, Karthik, and Nithin, Kumar turned his attention to Varun, who was another suspect in the murder case. During his interrogation, Varun revealed that he was heavily in debt and had been drinking and gambling excessively, leading to significant financial losses for his family. Varun's wife suggested that he should ask Venkatesh for financial assistance, which he did, and Venkatesh agreed to lend him the money on the condition that he would stop drinking and gambling.

Varun explained to Kumar that Venkatesh had helped him out of a difficult situation and had been like a god to him. He couldn't fathom why he would kill someone who had been so generous to him. Kumar considered Varun's story, but the large sum of money that had been transferred to his account remained suspicious.

With no clear evidence against any of the suspects, Kumar continued to dig deeper and explore every possible angle of the case. He knew that there was something more significant at play, and he was determined to uncover the truth behind Venkatesh's death. As he continued his investigation, he considered every detail, trying to connect the dots and piece together what had happened on that fateful day.

Kumar knew that Charan was a crucial suspect in the case, and he needed to investigate him thoroughly. The next day, he returned to Charan's office and began his investigation by examining all of the CCTV footage from his company to see if he could find any information related to Venkatesh's murder. He also reached out to Charan's close friends and business partners to gather more information and learn more about his character.

Kumar dug deeper into Charan's financial records, including his bank details, but nothing seemed to be out of place. He checked for any suspicious transactions or large sums of money transferred to his account, but everything appeared to be normal. Despite his extensive efforts, Kumar was unable to find any evidence to suggest that Charan was involved in Venkatesh's death.

Kumar scrutinized the CCTV footage in Raj's company and noticed that Nithin's appearance had dramatically improved after Venkatesh's death, which raised suspicions about his involvement in the murder case.

After interrogation, Nithin explained to Kumar that he was approached by a rival company that offered him a large sum of money in exchange for sensitive information about Venkatesh's business operations. Nithin was initially hesitant, but his financial difficulties and desire for a better life led him to agree to the offer. He started providing confidential information about Venkatesh's company to the rival company through encrypted channels, which eventually led to the downfall of Venkatesh's business.

Kumar was shocked to hear this and immediately arrested Nithin for corporate espionage. However, Nithin maintained that he was not responsible for Venkatesh's murder and had no knowledge of who might have done it. Kumar decided to continue his investigation to find out the real culprit behind the heinous crime. He knew that he had to be meticulous and methodical in his approach, as there were many people involved in the case and any wrong move could lead to a dead end.

5.THE UNCOVERING OF THE TRUTH

Kumar's investigation was beginning to take shape as he connected the dots and realized that the downfall of Raj's company was not a coincidence, but rather a well-planned scheme. He continued his investigation by interrogating Arun and other employees, who revealed that Ajay had the motive to become the CEO of the company but was passed over in favor of Raj. Armed with this information, Kumar decided to start monitoring Ajay's activities more closely and began tapping his phone. As he watched closely, he hoped to gather more evidence that would help him solve the case and bring the culprits to justice.

After some days, Ajay had a call from Charan. In the conversation, Charan asked if everything was okay Ajay replayed yeah everything is okay. Kumar realized that this was a major breakthrough in the case. He quickly worked to gather more evidence against Ajay and Charan. He obtained search warrants for their homes and offices and confiscated their computers and other electronic devices. After analyzing the data on these devices, he was able to find concrete proof that they were involved in the murder of Venkatesh.

In their electronic communications, Ajay and Charan had discussed their plans to take over Raj's company and had even discussed the possibility of killing Venkatesh. They also discussed their financial arrangements, including the transfer of funds in the form of crypto. With this evidence, Kumar was able to build a strong case against them.

When Ajay and Charan were brought in for questioning, they initially denied any involvement in the murder. However, when presented with the evidence against them, they both confessed to their crimes. They revealed that they had bribed Nithin to provide them with confidential information about Venkatesh's company and that they had conspired to murder Venkatesh in order to eliminate him as a competitor.

Ajay and Charan were both arrested and charged with murder, conspiracy, and various other crimes. The case was hailed as a major success for Kumar and his team and sent a strong message that such criminal activities would not be tolerated in society.

Raj felt an immense sense of relief and joy as he learned that his father's murderers had been caught and sent to jail. With this burden lifted, he was able to refocus his attention on his company's development. Through sheer determination and hard work, Raj was able to propel the company to the top position once again. His happiness was not only a result of his personal success but also the knowledge that justice had been served.